Written by Ellen Bailey

**Edited by Jen Wainwright
Designed by Zoe Quayle
Production by Joanne Rooke**

Picture Acknowledgements

Yui Mok/PA Archive/Press Association Images: Front cover; Rex Features: Back cover;
Dave Hogan/Getty Images: pages 2–3, 62–63;
Shirlaine Forrest/WireImage/Getty Images: pages 6, 15, 17, 19, 21, 34–35;
Doug Peters/EMPICS Entertainmen/Press Association Images: pages 8–9, 44, 45, 46;
Rex Features: pages 10, 12, 28–29;
Lewis Whyld/PA Archive/Press Association Images: page 11;
John Phillips/EMPICS Entertainment/Press Association Images: pages 22–23, 25;
Matt Kent/WireImage/Getty Images: page 24;
Nigel French/EMPICS Sport/Press Association Images: pages 30–31, 56–57;
Matt Crossick/EMPICS Entertainment/Press Association Images: pages 40–41
Raymond Boyd/Michael Ochs Archives/Getty Images: pages 48–49;
Guy Levy/EMPICS Entertainment/Press Association Images: pages 50–51;
Ian West/PA Wire/Press Association Images: Page 53;
Richard Young/Rex Features: Page 59;
Jon Furniss/WireImage/Getty Images: page 60
ShutterStock Inc: Images on page 31, background graphics on pages 5, 6–7, 8–9, 10–11, 12–13, 14–15, 16–17, 18–19,
20–21, 22–23, 24–25, 26–27, 30–31, 32–33, 36–37, 38–39, 40–41, 44–45, 46–47, 50–51, 52–53, 54–55, 58–59, 60–61.

Published in Great Britain in 2011 by Buster Books,
an imprint of Michael O'Mara Books Limited,
9 Lion Yard, Tremadoc Road, London SW4 7NQ

www.mombooks.com/busterbooks

Copyright © Buster Books 2011

A CIP catalogue record for this book is available from the British Library.

ISBN: 978-1-907151-79-8

PLEASE NOTE: This book is not affiliated with or endorsed by JLS or any of their publishers or licensees.

1 3 5 7 9 10 8 6 4 2

This book was printed in July 2011 by L.E.G.O., Viale dell'Industria 2, 36100, Vicenza, Italy.

By buying products with an FSC label you are supporting the growth of responsible forest management worldwide.
Papers used by Michael O'Mara Books are natural, recyclable products made from wood grown in sustainable
forests. The manufacturing processes conform to the environmental regulations of the country of origin.

JLS

ANNUAL 2012

UNAUTHORIZED

Buster Books

Contents

Outta This World

It was only right that JLS called their second album *Outta This World,* as that's exactly what life is now like for the band.

They've come a long way since auditioning as *X Factor* hopefuls in 2008. Today, VIP parties, red-carpet appearances, award ceremonies, stadium tours, photoshoots and screaming fans are all in a day's work for the boys.

Oritsé, Marvin, Aston and JB have back-flipped their way to superstardom and become the hottest boy band on the planet.

Staying Grounded

The boys haven't let fame go to their heads. They're still as down to earth as they were before they found fame – back when Oritsé was

applying to be a postman and Aston was working in a phone shop!

"To be honest we try not to think about the fame because then you get above your station," says Aston, modestly. "It's best to try not to get sucked into the hype too much.

It's about the music and everything else is a bonus."

Backstage Pass

In this book, you'll find out more about the music, the fame and the glittering lifestyle. Read on to discover what the boys have been up to over the past roller-coaster year, and find out what they really think about fashion, food, fans, fame and much, much more!

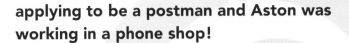

Shout Out To The JLSters

Did you know that you, yes you, keep the JLS boys smiling? The band love performing, but it's the happy faces and excited screams from fans like you that make the boys want to dance harder, sing better and show off their buff bodies more!

"We can't thank them enough, you know," says JB of their fans. "Those guys have put us where we are. We say it all the time and people think it's a cliché, but it's the truth."

The JLS boys know what it's like to be a super-fan, too. All four of them love Michael Jackson's music and remember the excitement of seeing him in concert. Oritsé even remembers running after Jackson's car and banging on the window! The lads know how it feels to wait all day to catch a glimpse of your fave pop star, so they make sure they always spend as much time with their fans as possible.

When JLS were writing songs for their first album, they wanted to write something special for their supporters and that's when they came up with 'Close To You'. It's dedicated to the fans, because for these four boys, no one comes close to a JLSter.

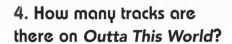

Ultimate Fan Quiz

Take this quiz to put your JLS knowledge to the test and prove your super-fan status to the world! Find the answers on page 61.

1. JLS were originally called UFO. What does it stand for?

A. **Unbelievable Fantastic Original**

B. Ultimate Fresh Onstage

C. Unique Famous Outrageous

D. Us Four OK

2. The boys won their first award in 2007 for Best Unsigned Act. Which award ceremony was it?

A. Urban Music Awards

B. **BRIT Awards**

C. MOBO Awards

D. Virgin Media Music Awards

3. 'The Club Is Alive' includes a sample from which musical?

A. *High School Musical*

B. *Grease*

C. *The Lion King*

D. **The Sound of Music**

4. How many tracks are there on *Outta This World*?

A. 10

B. **13**

C. 14

D. 17

5. JLS's debut single went straight into the British charts at number one. What was the name of the track?

A. 'Everybody In Love'

B. **'Beat Again'**

C. 'The Club is Alive'

D. 'Crazy For You'

6. Which recording artist features on the JLS track 'Eyes Wide Shut'?

A. Tinchy Stryder

B. Tinie Tempah

C. **Usher**

D. Lemar

★11★

Superheroes

Being in a boy band as big as JLS isn't all about private jets, amazing parties and adoring fans. OK, it is about that a bit, but it also takes a superhuman amount of determination, dedication and talent.

Hard At Work

While the boys do take time to enjoy the benefits of being super-successful, they're not the kind of people to sit back, relax and think 'we've made it'. They are always aiming higher, working harder and striving for better.

This means spending long days learning dance routines and recording in the studio. Not only do the boys work hard on their slick moves and silky-smooth harmonies – the creative cuties also wrote nine of the thirteen tracks on their debut album, and all but 'The Club Is Alive' on *Outta This World*. Impressive stuff!

Chasing The Dream

The lads put their hearts and souls into everything they do and you can hear it in their music. "It's important for our fans to know that our take on everything we perform is very true because we've written it," says Marvin.

Back when they were in the X Factor house Aston, Oritsé, JB and Marvin wrote a list of 300 things that they wanted to achieve – both individually and as a band. Sure enough, week by week, the determined lads are ticking things off the list!

Use this notepad to write down your own list of goals and get ready to start making your dreams come true! There are some suggestions to help you get started.

One day I will win an award for ....

I want to be the best at ....

In ten years' time I will be ....

I want to learn how to ....

Add more of your own hopes and ambitions below:

....

....

....

....

....

We Heart Oritsé

Leader Of The Pack

As the founder of the band, Oritsé is the driving force behind JLS. Super-ambitious from a very young age, Oritsé has been plotting world domination for as long as he can remember.

It was his vision of a seriously talented, ultra-cool boy band that led him to Aston, Marvin and JB. Oritsé spotted a unique blend of charisma, singing ability, star quality and dedication in each of the boys and he knew that he had found his dream team.

Over the past year, JLS have won award after award, dominated the British charts, and performed with some of the biggest stars in the industry. "Every day I have to pinch myself," said Oritsé recently. "This is closer than I ever could've imagined to the original idea for JLS."

Full Focus

Oritsé is from a family with high expectations and he always pushes for perfection – nothing less will do! He loves recording songs in studios located in the countryside, because the isolation means that there are no distractions and the boys can really focus on their work.

Among Oritsé's musical influences are Stevie Wonder, Michael Jackson and Usher, and you can be sure that he won't stop until JLS are as big as his idols. In fact, he won't stop until JLS are the biggest band on Earth.

Fun Fact:

The boys at Oritsé's school gave him a hard time for his love of singing. But as they got older and all the girls started being interested in Oritsé, they soon realized that he was on to something!

All About Aston

Party Animal

Aston says that if he were an animal he'd be a little monkey and with his cheeky grin and playful nature you can see why. Aston loves to play practical jokes on people – he caused havoc when he put plastic wrap over the toilet seat on the JLS tour bus!

Always the life and soul of every party, Aston is a massive hit with the ladies. "If I had to say which one of us gets the most action, I'd go with Aston," says bandmate Marvin. "He definitely gets the most attention from our fans."

Alter Ego

When Aston goes on stage he switches into an alter ego that walks differently, talks differently and even smiles differently than the off-stage Aston. "It's hard to express how it works," he says. "It's like, light on, light off."

The adrenaline kicks in and he's often so into the whole experience that he doesn't even remember it after the performance.

Seriously Sporty

Aston has always been into athletics and at school he took part in the 100 metres, 200 metres, 4 x 100 metres relay, long jump and triple jump. He even competed in athletics for Great Britain in Germany.

Aston says that he shouldn't have to write his signature when he goes to the bank, he should just do a back flip, as that's his signature move ... geddit?

Fun Fact:

When he was a child, Aston wowed the audience as a young Michael Jackson on the TV show *Stars In Their Eyes*, where performers impersonate their musical idols.

Marvin's The Man

A Born Performer

Marvin made his singing debut at his brother's christening when he was just seven years old. He performed Shaggy's 'Oh Carolina' and the crowd went wild. Ever since then, he has known that performing was what he was destined to do. A few years later, he got his first all-singing, all-dancing job playing one of Fagin's boys in the West End musical *Oliver!* and he hasn't looked back since.

Clean Machine

Sensible Marvin is obsessed with things being clean and tidy. He likes everything to be organized and lines up all his clothes and aftershaves in perfect order. Everything in his bedroom is white and cream – he even has a white TV and a white DVD player. So if you ever get a chance to go to Marvin's house, make sure you take off your shoes so you don't mess up the cream carpet!

In The Limelight

Marvin loves the attention that comes with being in JLS, but it can sometimes be difficult to have your love life and most personal experiences splashed on the pages of newspapers. Marvin says that his bedroom is his haven. He likes being able to go in there and shut the door, knowing that he can completely relax and get some peace and quiet.

Fun Fact:

Marvin starred in 14 episodes of the TV hospital drama *Holby City* as the character Robbie Waring.

Crazy For JB

A Way With Words

Hitting the studio and getting down to some serious song writing is JB's favourite part of the job. He has loved reading and writing from a young age and was one of the top pupils in his English class at school. Writing with JLS is a dream come true for the talented star. One of his ambitions is to write songs for other bestselling recording artists from all over the world. Brainy JB was studying for a degree at a university in London before JLS hit the heights of superstardom and he still plans to complete his studies one day.

Catching Some Zzzzzzzzs

Of all the members of JLS, JB is the most likely to be caught with his eyes wide shut. There's nothing he loves more than to snuggle into a comfy bed with freshly laundered sheets – ideally yellow ones!

JB needs at least eight hours sleep per night and would like to retire at 35 to spend more time in the land of nod.

Up Close And Personal

JB loves to be romantic and surprise girlfriends with thoughtful presents and dreamy dates. For JB, taking time and taking care of each other is at the heart of building a strong relationship.

JB doesn't have a particular type of girl he goes for. He likes girls who know their own minds and can think for themselves.

Fun Fact:

Not only is he an incredible singer, with a real gift for harmonies, but JB can also play the flute and the piano.

Eyes Wide Shut

JLS and hip-hop rapper Tinie Tempah had been talking about collaborating for ages. They were just waiting for the right track. As soon as Tinie heard 'Eyes Wide Shut', he knew that the time had come: "They finally found a song that I could be on, and that was amazing. It was nice to finally be a part of it."

Tinie's Talent

Tinie Tempah (aka Patrick Chukwuemeka Okogwu Jr) has rocketed to success in a very short period of time, just like the JLS boys, and he's equally determined to succeed. "I want people to see this is not a joke to me. Now I'm here and I've been given the opportunity, I'm not messing around. I'm looking to take my tour, the videos, the music, everything, completely beyond what you can fathom. It's never just another day in the life of Tinie. I've got a lot to do, and you can bet on the fact that I'll do it."

Tinie's honest, witty lyrics combined with slick beats have earned him respect from critics and adoration from fans. His rap definitely brought something fresh to the remix of JLS's club track. The boys love it. "This, right here, is history," grins Oritsé. "I'm so proud to be in JLS right now, collaborating with Tinie Tempah."

Kiss The Girls

The video features JLS and Tinie Tempah in a computer-generated fantasy world. While Tinie looks dapper in a suit and his trademark glasses, the boys chase a girl who disappears every time they get close.

The lads admit that they do sometimes fall a little in love with their video girls. During the shoot for 'Everybody In Love', Oritsé even had a kiss! "The directors started saying, 'Ooh!' and wolf-whistling and all

sorts," remembers Oritsé. "Then it happened again. Everyone was like, 'OK, now calm down, guys. This is a video, not real life.'"

Green Screen Scene

On the 'Eyes Wide Shut' shoot, the boys didn't know what the video would look like until they saw the finished product. "It's all green screen, so there's no actual props or anything. It's just us, our outfits and the music," explains Aston. The result was a breathtaking, cutting-edge music video.

Now the lads are keen to link up with other artists. Their favourites are Stevie Wonder, Usher, Beyoncé and Justin Timberlake. So who knows what the future will hold …

Super Stars

JLS have their fair share of superstar fans. Can you match each of the quotes below to the superstar who said them? Then take a look at the things the JLS boys have said on the opposite page and work out which stars they were talking about. Check your answers on page 61.

The Stars On JLS

1. "They put on a class performance and I think they will go on to be as big as *N Sync."

2. "The JLS boys are great and I'd love to be the fifth member."

3. "I think they might break America. There's a buzz."

4. "They caused some early Take That hysteria among young girls. All my young girlfriends absolutely love them. Mothers love them. They appeal to women I think, and they're able to cause that hysteria with a big performance."

5. "They can sing, they can dance, they look good. Actually they look very good."

Cheryl Cole

Simon Cowell

Peter Andre

Jay-Z

Rihanna

JLS On The Stars

6. "He is the most humble guy. He's always so respectful and I think that transcends through his songs." (JB)

7. "He has been the biggest influence on JLS musically." (Marvin)

8. "She heard it and said that she really likes it, which is incredible – to hear it from the lady herself!" (Marvin)

9. "She's gone from strength to strength. She's a great talent and a great vocalist." (JB)

10. "I'm very driven and ambitious in the same way he is, and I'd love to emulate his success. I've watched all the documentaries about him and I've seen how hard he works." (Oritsé)

Pixie Lott

Julie Andrews

Michael Jackson

Tinie Tempah

Jay-Z

Style Update

When JLS were first taking part in *The X Factor*, the individual colours they wore were their trademark. The boys looked super-cute in their coloured hoodies – Oritsé in red, Aston in blue, JB in yellow and Marvin in green. The JLS wardrobe was stocked full of clothes in the boys' colours: T-shirts, leather jackets – even underwear!

The Next Level

In the time since they've become chart-busting sensations, the lads have swapped large blocks of colour, such as the hoodies and T-shirts, for more subtle accessories in their trademark colours. This has given them the freedom to explore and develop their own unique styles, while staying true to their original look.

The lads think carefully about the clothes that they wear and how they work

together. "Even when we're just chilling in the house we like to be together as much as possible and make sure there is something going on between all of us and that we're all connected," says Marvin.

In the style stakes, the boys admire Jude Law, Dizzee Rascal, Rio Ferdinand and David Beckham. Aston even admits to copying Mr Beckham when he wore a sarong on holiday!

Trendsetters

The boys have rocked the fashion world with their updated style. The low V-necked T-shirts that Marvin loves to wear are now a stylish must-have. And JB's been doing his bit, too, with his sharp and suave look. "Nobody rocked the bow tie in pop music till JB did in 'Beat Again'," says Oritsé.

The Accessories Test

For JLS, style is all about the accessories. They finish a look and allow you to express your personality in a unique way.

Choose the accessory from the pictures below that is most important to your signature style, then turn to pages 32 and 33 to find out what it says about you.

A Fedora

Sunglasses

Dog Tags

A Classic Watch

Diamond Studs

A Neck Scarf

A Bright Belt

Colourful Trainers

A Suave Tie

Your Style File

Find out what the accessory you chose on page 31 says about your personality and your signature style.

A Fedora

You're outgoing and ambitious and you love to be the centre of attention. Like Oritsé, you know how to rock a decent hat. "They have to be a certain kind of hat, at a certain angle, or else it won't work," he advises.

A Bright Belt

You've got a great sense of humour and you like to express this in your clothes. You and Aston share a secret – you know that the best accessory you can have is a gorgeous smile.

A Classic Watch

You're classy and sophisticated and you know your own mind. Like JB, you dress well and believe it's important to take a lot of time and care over your appearance.

Sunglasses

Your air of mystery is important to your image. You have the 'X' factor and will be successful no matter what you choose to do. Like Marvin, you value privacy and know that a pair of shades is the perfect accessory to hide behind.

Colourful Trainers

You're sporty, full of energy and you're always ready for anything. It's important that your clothes and accessories don't restrict you as, like Aston, you may be required to do a back flip at any time.

Diamond Studs

You have a taste for the finer things in life and make sure you always look your best. You're a perfectionist and, like Oritsé, you look in the mirror a hundred times before you leave the house!

A Neck Scarf

People often comment on your outfits and ask where you picked up your accessories. Like Marvin, you're not afraid to take risks and your individual style gets you noticed.

A Suave Tie

You're a trendsetter with a passion for fashion. You're always one step ahead of the game and, like JB, your friends look to you when they want to know what's hot and what's not.

Dog Tags

You're honest and open and you like to keep things simple, with a punchy dog-tag necklace. Like all the JLS boys, you're keen to stamp your own style on your outfits, so why not get a cool engraving that's totally personal to you?

A Day With JLS

Answer the questions and follow this flow chart to spend a day with JLS. At the end of it you'll find out which of the lads you have the most in common with.

Just go with the flow ...

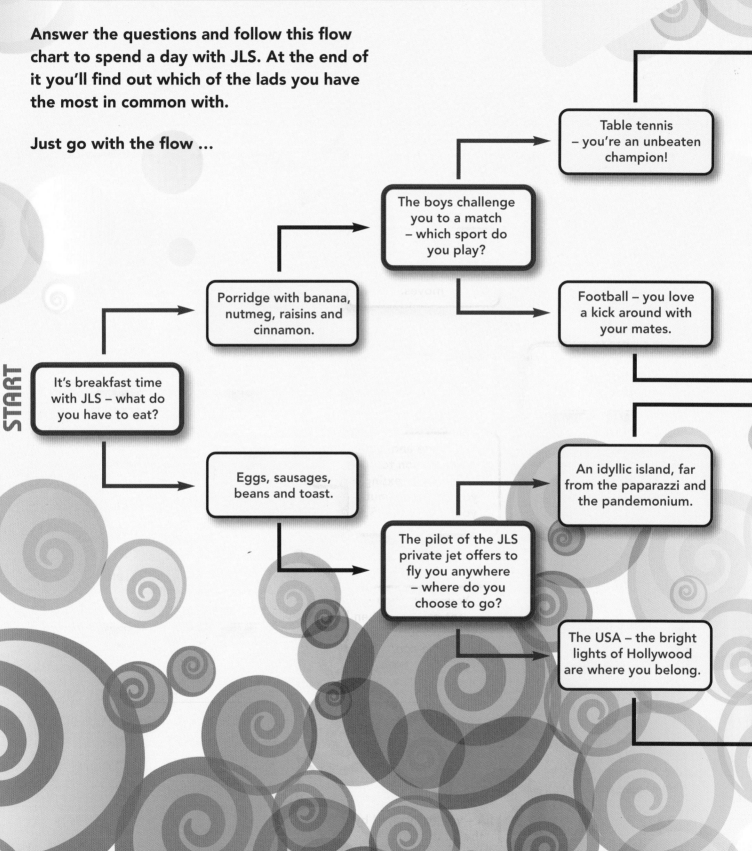

START

It's breakfast time with JLS – what do you have to eat?

Porridge with banana, nutmeg, raisins and cinnamon.

Eggs, sausages, beans and toast.

The boys challenge you to a match – which sport do you play?

Table tennis – you're an unbeaten champion!

Football – you love a kick around with your mates.

The pilot of the JLS private jet offers to fly you anywhere – where do you choose to go?

An idyllic island, far from the paparazzi and the pandemonium.

The USA – the bright lights of Hollywood are where you belong.

You kick back and watch a movie with the boys – which film gets your vote?

High School Musical – you love a good old singsong.

Titanic – romantic movies are more your thing.

Oritsé

Genuine and friendly Oritsé is your JLS best mate. You've both got a competitive streak and a great sense of humour to go with it. A day spent with him is sure to end in fits of giggles.

Marvin

You've got most in common with down-to-earth Marvin. You're organized and practical, and always ready to party. Secretly though, you're both real softies.

It's midnight. What do you and the lads do next?

Turn up the stereo and get ready to bust out your best dance moves.

Head home and resist the temptation to stay up all night texting your friends about your day with JLS.

Your room. You concentrate best when you're surrounded by your home comforts.

JB

You're just like JB. You're fun to be around and are great at making people feel at ease, but you're happiest when you're chilling out at home with family, good friends and good food.

Aston

Cheeky chappy Aston is the JLS guy who's most like you. You're both pint-sized whirlwinds of energy and you're always ready with a joke and a smile to keep everyone in high spirits.

You've been asked to co-write a song with JLS. Where do you head to get down to work?

LA – you're inspired by the buzz of the city.

OMG ... JLS in 3D!

Eyes Wide Open, JLS's fab concert movie, meant that you didn't have to go to a live show to see the lads in 3D! Full of rippling biceps, awesome dance moves and, of course, the ultimate JLS soundtrack, the movie was a must-see for all fans.

Branching Out

Making the movie was a big deal for the lads, who wanted to push themselves creatively and branch out. "Obviously, we love our music, and that will always be our base, but we love to do other things which are in the creative realm," explains Oritsé. "We feel very strongly about doing things that we feel passionate about, and also things that we're capable of doing. Two of the boys come from stage-school backgrounds, and acting is certainly something that we're comfortable doing."

Born To Perform

Aston gained confidence in front of the camera as a character called Cookie on children's TV show *The Fun Song Factory*. "It was a good experience for me," he grins. "I did it for three years and I was only 15 when I began. It taught me a lot. I'm not scared of an audience, and the camera doesn't bother me either."

Before joining JLS, Marvin had also worked as an actor. At the age of ten he saw an advertisement for D&B School of Performing Arts and begged his mum and dad to let him attend. Although money was tight his parents agreed to let him go and their investment in his future certainly paid off.

While still at school, Marvin appeared in several TV shows and on stage in a West End musical. "It was the best training for me and really helped me develop and learn my craft as a performer," says Marvin. "It's so important to have an all round understanding of performing arts because in this day and age you have to be so versatile."

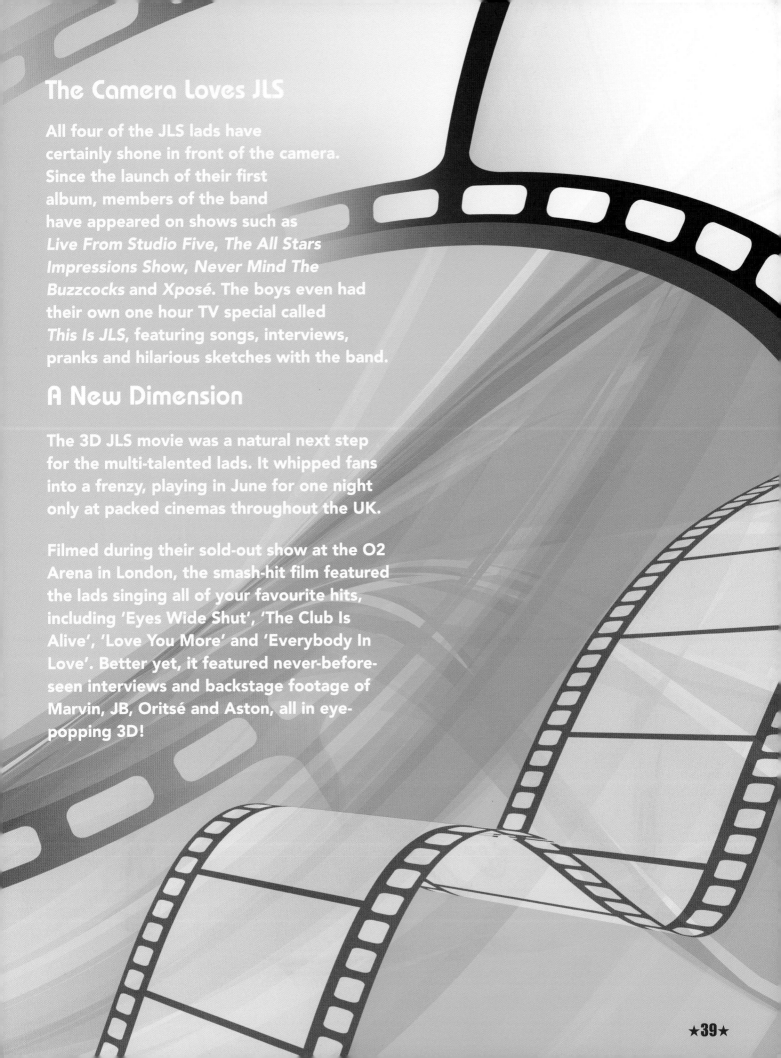

The Camera Loves JLS

All four of the JLS lads have certainly shone in front of the camera. Since the launch of their first album, members of the band have appeared on shows such as *Live From Studio Five*, *The All Stars Impressions Show*, *Never Mind The Buzzcocks* and *Xposé*. The boys even had their own one hour TV special called *This Is JLS*, featuring songs, interviews, pranks and hilarious sketches with the band.

A New Dimension

The 3D JLS movie was a natural next step for the multi-talented lads. It whipped fans into a frenzy, playing in June for one night only at packed cinemas throughout the UK.

Filmed during their sold-out show at the O2 Arena in London, the smash-hit film featured the lads singing all of your favourite hits, including 'Eyes Wide Shut', 'The Club Is Alive', 'Love You More' and 'Everybody In Love'. Better yet, it featured never-before-seen interviews and backstage footage of Marvin, JB, Oritsé and Aston, all in eye-popping 3D!

What's In A Name?

You probably know that JLS stands for Jack The Lad Swing, but do you know where the boys' names are from and what each name means?

First Name: Oritsé
Meaning: You are universally blessed
Origin: Nigerian
Surname: Williams
Nicknames: Glitzy Ritzy, Music Boy, Reesh, O, Nightwalker

First Name: Aston
Meaning: East town
Origin: Old English
Surname: Merrygold
Nicknames: Lil' Man, Ast, Boy Blue, A.S.

Complete your own name file here:
First Name: ....
Meaning: ....
Origin: ....
Surname: ....
Nicknames: ....
....

First Name: Marvin
Meaning: Sea friend
Origin: Welsh
Surname: Humes
Nicknames: Marv, Desh, Oblong Head, Petrol

First Names: Jonathan Benjamin (JB)
Meaning: Gift of God
Origin: Hebrew
Surname: Gill
Nicknames: Gilly, Gillster, Jaybes, JG

★41★

Love You More

For JLS, being pop stars is about more than just entertaining people. The lads understand that their celeb status gives them the power to be able to make a difference in the world using more than just their music. The big-hearted boys use their fame to raise money for charities and put out messages about important issues.

Spreading Smiles

"We are in the fortunate position of being able to lift people's spirits when they are ill or feeling down," says Marvin. "A couple of minutes spent by a hospital bed can make such a huge difference."

Four Times The Love

Not only does the band as a whole put time and effort into supporting those in need, each of the boys also supports a charity that is close to his heart. Read on to discover more about the charities that the lads work with and how they really do love you more ...

Oritsé And The MS Society

When Oritsé was 12 years old, his mum was diagnosed with a medical condition called Multiple Sclerosis (MS) that affects the nerves and can make doing ordinary things very difficult. Oritsé had to play a big part in looking after his mum, his sister and his brothers. "I actually put my band together because I was trying to find a way of helping my mum," he says. "I thought if I try and become a pop star or something like that then maybe I can get some money and give my mum a better environment."

Oritsé has done a lot of work supporting other young carers in the same position and even won the MS Inspiration Award in 2010.

Marvin And The NSPCC

The National Society for the Prevention of Cruelty to Children is Marvin's charity of choice. He has helped to launch ChildLine's 'How U Feelin?' online campaign. "I'm really proud to support ChildLine and to help launch its great new website that lets children express their feelings and get help for their problems," he says.

"Everyone has bad days, even pop stars. When I'm touring with JLS it can get stressful and I miss my family, but talking to my bandmates about it makes me feel better. When children find it difficult to talk about their feelings and problems to their friends and family, ChildLine is there for them."

Aston And Beatbullying

Aston was bullied at school by members of his football team. "When you first start out in a team, you have a laugh, and all mates take the mick out of each other, but it got to the point where they'd be making jokes about things that were irrelevant. Skin colour started coming into it. It was hurtful," he says.

Aston is now an ambassador for Beatbullying, a charity that works with children who are being bullied. "It's important for me personally," Aston says. "Kids being bullied need the message that they're not alone."

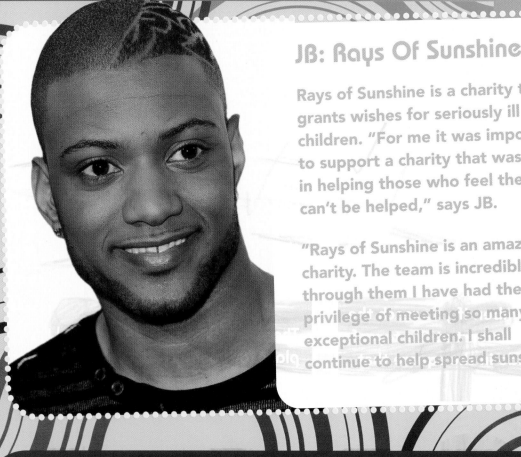

JB: Rays Of Sunshine

Rays of Sunshine is a charity that grants wishes for seriously ill children. "For me it was important to support a charity that was active in helping those who feel they can't be helped," says JB.

"Rays of Sunshine is an amazing charity. The team is incredible and through them I have had the privilege of meeting so many exceptional children. I shall continue to help spread sunshine."

Alphabetter

Tinie Tempah has got hold of JLS's set list and rearranged the letters. Can you unscramble the song titles in time for the concert? Check your answers on page 61.

1. ETH BULC SI EIVAL

2. SYEE WDIE UHST

3. KWOR

4. EVLO OYU MROE

5. OREHPSUER

6. ETAB INAGA

7. ENO TOSH

8. VPRTAEI

9. ON'DT OG

10. SCITTKARK

11. OGHTREITP

12. HTE SALT GONS

Ultimate JLS Experience

Follow the instructions below to discover what your ultimate evening with JLS would be like!

1. Count the number of letters in your favourite JLS colour. Subtract this number from your age. Then add ten to the total. This is your JLS number.

2. Starting at the top of the left-hand column of the grid below, count down the column boxes, and stop when you reach your JLS number. If you reach the bottom of a column, start at the top of the next one. Shade in the square that you land on.

3. From the shaded square, count up to your JLS number again. When you get to the bottom of the fourth column, start again at the top of the first column.

4. Keep counting down the column boxes, skipping any squares that you have shaded. Shade in a square every time you hit your number, and keep going until there is just one unmarked box in each column.

These last four boxes will reveal the plans for your incredible evening with JLS. Are you ready for some fun?

You get an invite from ...	To a JLS concert, including ...	Followed by ...	With JLS and ...
Oritsé	A red carpet walk	Dancing at an A-list party	Tinie Tempah
JB	Front row seats	A fancy dinner	The Saturdays
Aston	A backstage pass	A midnight swim	Simon Cowell
Marvin	An on stage cameo	A live performance in your living room	Your Best Mate

The Food of Love

"Food is a subject that's close to our hearts. We are bigger foodies than any other musicians you'll meet," says Oritsé. When they were in the X Factor house, the boys would regularly cook up delicious meals for their housemates.

Nice And Spicy For Oritsé!

Oritsé's speciality is Thai green curry. He grew up eating good, fresh food and it's important to him to watch what he puts into his body. When he's in training for a tour he always has a

Did You Know?

If there's one thing the boys all agree on it's the restaurant Nando's. If they can't agree on what to have for dinner, that's where they'll head! Aston even uses it as a first date test – if a girl likes Nando's, she's off to a good start!

nutritious, healthy breakfast, and then plenty of protein and fresh vegetables during the day. Oritsé likes almost everything, even things that a lot of other people don't eat. He spent time in Tobago when he was younger and would fish for crabs with his brother and cook them up to make crab-meat soup.

Adventurous Marvin

Like Oritsé, Marvin loves to cook with fresh ingredients and one of the hardest things about being on tour is having to grab convenience food on the go. He admires the style and freshness of Japanese food and his favourite dish is black miso cod. He's an adventurous eater and loves exploring exotic cuisines.

JB And The Sea

JB is a seafood man, too, and he loves to eat fresh shellfish on the beach. He adores the taste of the Caribbean and his great-aunt makes a mean Caribbean soup. "It's soooo good," he says. "You put anything in there and I'd eat it."

Fussy Aston

Aston, on the other hand, is a fussy eater. When he was growing up his mum would often have to cook him a whole separate dinner, and the only vegetables he'll eat are peas and carrots. His fridge is stocked up with all different types of fruit juice to make sure he gets his five a day.

Aston's acrobatics are fuelled by ketchup, which he pours over everything. He'd always rather have an extra portion of meat instead of the vegetables, double burger to start followed by a full rack of ribs and fries for the main course? No problem ... just don't forget the ketchup!

What They Want

Here are some of the things the boys insist on having on their 'rider' list, which is the list of things that they need before a concert. Can you find all the things in the list below in the wordsearch grid? The words are hidden forwards, backwards, upwards, downwards and even diagonally. Check your answers on page 61.

Hair Gel Vitamin C Aftershave

Mouthwash Toothbrushes Throat Sweets

Sunglasses Deodorant Boxer Shorts Lip Balm

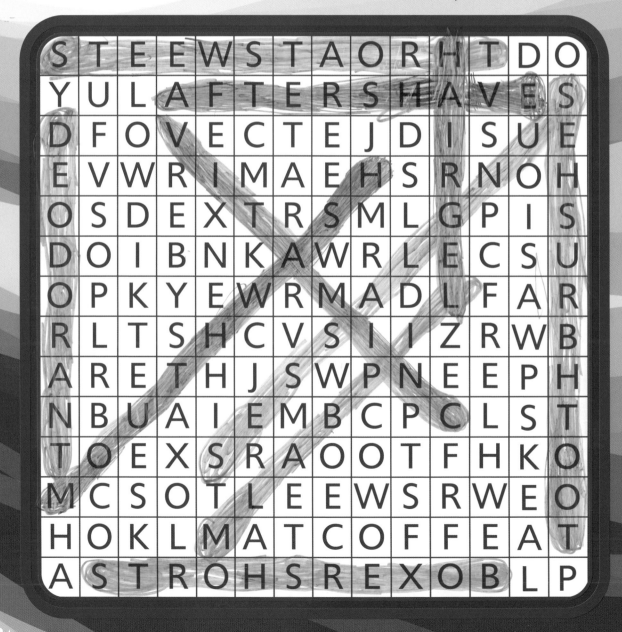

S T E E W S T A O R H T D O
Y U L A F T E R S H A V E S
D F O V E C T E J D I S U E
E V W R I M A E H S R N O H
O S D E X T R S M L G P I S
D O I B N K A W R L E C S U
O P K Y E W R M A D L F A R
R L T S H C V S I I Z R W B
A R E T H J S W P N E E P H
N B U A I E M B C P C P L S T
T O E X S R A O O T F H K O
M C S O T L E E W S R W E O
H O K L M A T C O F F E A T
A S T R O H S R E X O B L P

JLS To LAX

The JLS boys have got a flight to catch from the airport in Los Angeles, which is known as LAX.

Place one coin for each player on the START square and use a dice to race from the hotel to the airport.

First to the finish gets to fly in swanky first class, but beware, if you're the last one to the airport you'll miss your flight.

START

A photographer is chasing you. Roll again to get away.

Your taxi driver knows a short cut. Jump ahead two spaces.

Ouch! You have toothache and need to see a dentist. Miss a turn.

You're distracted by a new restaurant and stop for lunch. Miss two turns while you munch your food.

You drop your passport. Move back three spaces to find it.

FINISH

There's a fan hiding in one of your bags! Miss a turn while security search the rest of your luggage.

★54★

You back flip over the Hollywood sign – jump ahead three spaces!

You stop to sign some autographs. Miss a turn.

The new trainers you bought help you run fast. Roll again.

You spot Jay-Z walking down the street. Miss a turn while you talk to him.

Other Side Of The World

JLS have always set their sights high and nothing short of world domination will be enough for the lads. "We're hungry for it," exclaims JB. "We want to get our music to as many places in the world as possible."

A New World

With the likes of Jay-Z and Simon Cowell tipping the boys as the next big thing in the States, JLS are on track to global superstardom. Having sold over one million copies of their debut album in just two months and with the tour selling out in under 24 hours, the boys headed overseas with one mission in mind – to crack America.

"Coming to the States this soon wasn't part of our plan," says Oritsé. "We hoped it might happen in a few years, maybe once we had broken Europe. Then radio stations started playing our music without knowing who we were. We were offered a deal and asked to come and meet the people supporting us."

Heading Stateside

The boys were signed by Jive Records, and released 'Everybody In Love' as their debut single in the USA. The trip to the states has been a highlight of the boys' career to date. They took in shopping on Rodeo Drive, video shoots, TV debuts, radio interviews, live performances, song-writing and some serious partying!

Chowing And Chilling

All the boys agree that one of the best things about being in LA was the food. The massive portions were just what the boys needed after a hard day's work. "You order ribs in London and you get four or five," says Aston. "In LA they serve the kind of portions I want for a meal!"

The boys loved the fact that they could all hang out together and do normal things such as go for a burger or mess around in the shopping mall without being swamped by the paparazzi. But they missed their British fans. "It's been a bit of a humbling experience, and it makes you massively appreciate what you've got back home," says Marvin.

Working Their Way To The USA

Unafraid of hard work, the boys are happy to do whatever it takes to get the Americans to put their hands up for JLS. "We'll do this for a year – or two or three, if that's what it takes. We'd rather do it right than rush it," says JB. "We're having the time of our lives and we're determined to enjoy every second of it."

Next For JLS

With a string of number one hits, countless music industry awards and even a 3D movie under their belts, JLS's speedy rise to superstardom continues without showing signs of stopping. The strength of the boys' friendship and their steely determination to succeed make them a force to be reckoned with.

Like everyone, the boys have had their fair share of ups and downs. It's not always easy to spend long periods of time away from home and they have each had to deal with difficulties in their personal lives, such as family illness. But the lads are always there to support each other no matter what's going on, and they know they can always rely on their bandmates to make them smile.

The boys have their feet firmly on the ground and never take what they've got for granted. Whether they're writing songs for their next album, speaking out for a cause they believe in, or meeting their fans, the boys never stop working. "There is always something new to achieve," says Aston. "There's always records to be broken. There's always new things to do. There's always something you can learn and be striving towards."

Wherever the boys decide to channel their energies next, you can be sure that they'll make a success of it. For JLS, there are very exciting times to come. The way things are going, Oritsé's ambition for "JLS to be the biggest band in the world" looks set to come true!

Answers

Ultimate Fan Quiz – Page 11

1. C
2. A
3. D
4. C
5. B
6. B

Super Stars – Pages 26 and 27

1. Jay-Z
2. Peter Andre
3. Simon Cowell
4. Cheryl Cole
5. Rihanna
6. Tinie Tempah
7. Michael Jackson
8. Julie Andrews
9. Pixie Lott
10. Jay-Z

Alphabetter – Page 46

1. The Club Is Alive
2. Eyes Wide Shut
3. Work
4. Love You More
5. Superhero
6. Beat Again
7. One Shot
8. Private
9. Don't Go
10. Kickstart
11. Tightrope
12. The Last Song

What They Want – Page 52.

```
S T E E W S T A O R H T D O
Y U L A F T E R S H A V E S
D F O V E C T E J D   S U E
E V W R I M A E H S R N O H
O S D E X T R S M L G P I S
D O I B N K A W R L E C S U
O P K Y E W R M A D L F A R
R L T S H C V S I I Z R W B
A R E T H J S W P N E E P H
N B U A I E M B C P O L S T
T O E X S R A O O T F H K O
M C S O T L E E W S R W E O
H O K L M A T C O F F E A T
A S T R O H S R E X O B L P
```